NATIONAL GEOGRAPHIC

Do Elephants Talk?

PIONEER EDITION

By Peter Winkler

CONTENTS

The day is hot. Elephants walk across the dry ground. They are very thirsty. The **herd,** or group, has been walking for miles. They are headed to a water hole. They are almost there.

Suddenly the elephants stop. All is quiet. Yet the elephants raise their ears. They seem to hear something. The adults move closer to their **calves,** or babies. Then the elephants turn and walk away. What did they hear?

SECRET LANGUAGE

The elephants heard a low sound. It is part of a secret language. Elephants use it to talk when they are far apart.

The low sound is called **infrasound.** It travels for miles. People cannot hear infrasound. It is too low for our ears. So how do we know about it?

People use machines to study infrasound. One machine records the elephants' sounds. Then another makes pictures of the sounds. The pictures let us see what the elephants are saying.

▶ **Family Gathering.**
Danger brings elephants together. The adults guard the young.

▲ **Real Nose-y.**
An elephant's trunk has 50,000 muscles. It works like an arm, hand, and fingers.

Do Elephants TALK?

Elephants are the largest land animals. They sometimes seem quiet. Yet these big beasts have a lot to say.

TEXT BY PETER WINKLER

TALKING IN THE WILD

Elephants make many sounds. They bark and roar. These sounds may be loud. Yet they do not travel far. Infrasound does. These messages help elephants keep in touch.

WARNING CALLS

Some messages help elephants stay safe. Remember the elephants near the water hole? They heard a **warning call.** That is a message about danger. Another herd may have sent the message. Maybe a lion was near. Lions can kill elephant calves. A drink was not worth the risk. So the herd turned away.

STAYING CLOSE

Some messages help keep families together. How? Elephants may walk many miles for food. Sometimes they go alone. Infrasound helps them find their families again. It brings the herd back together.

Other messages help elephant calves. Young elephants sometimes wander off. They can get into trouble. When that happens, they cry for help.

Adult elephants hear the baby's cry. They answer. They use infrasound. They say, "It is okay. We are coming to help you."

In the Wild. TOP: Lions attack elephant calves. So this elephant might warn herds to stay away. ABOVE: An adult can eat 300 pounds of leaves and grass in just one day.

Going Wild. Young elephants are playful. They like to be social. They cover themselves with mud in play. Mud blocks heat and flies.

HEARING AIDS

Elephant ears are good for catching sound. Elephants can stretch their ears out wide. This lets them hear many noises.

When an elephant listens, it also uses its trunk. That is its long nose. The elephant smells the air. This may help the elephant figure out what it is hearing.

ELEPHANTS IN DANGER

Elephants can hear when danger is near. Yet elephants are still having trouble staying alive. They may become **extinct,** or die out forever.

A million elephants once lived in Africa. Today, only about 500,000 live there. The number of wild elephants keeps getting smaller.

CALL FOR HELP

What is happening to the elephants? Some people kill them for their **tusks.** These long teeth are made of ivory. They can be sold for a lot of money.

Elephants are also losing their **habitats,** or homes. People build on land where elephants once lived.

Luckily, many people are working to save elephants. They are trying to stop the sale of ivory. They have also made parks. Elephants are safe there. This may help elephants survive.

WORDWise

calf: the young of some large animals, such as whales and elephants (plural: *calves*)

extinct: no longer alive on Earth

habitat: the place where something lives

herd: group of one type of animal that stays together

infrasound: sound so low that humans cannot hear it

tusk: long, ivory tooth that sticks out from an elephant's mouth

warning call: message about danger

Super

size

Really Tall
Really Tough
Really Big

Elephants are big. They are the largest land animals. They can be ten feet tall. They are heavy too. They weight up to 12,000 pounds!

Elephants have big bodies. Their ears, trunks, and tusks are huge. These parts are not just for show. They help elephants survive.

GOOD EARS

Elephants have good ears. They hear even tiny sounds. They can hear when a lion is near. Good hearing helps an elephant stay alive.

Ears also help an elephant stay cool. How? They are giant fans in hot weather. An elephant stirs up a breeze with its ears.

Big Beasts. Elephants are the planet's largest land animals.

A NEAT NOSE

Trunks are useful too. Elephants use them to eat and drink. They use them to smell. They also use them to talk.

An elephant's trunk has lots of muscles. It is strong. It can lift fallen trees. But it does small jobs too. It can pick up tiny leaves and twigs. Imagine having a nose that could do all that!

TOUGH TEETH

An elephant also has strong teeth. Its longest teeth are called tusks.

Elephants use their tusks as tools. They can dig with them. They can even use them to pull up trees. Tusks are powerful tools!

Teeth, trunks, and ears are useful. Each part of an elephant's body helps it survive in the wild.

Ecosystems
and Elephants

Elephants are large. They play a big role in the ecosystem. An ecosystem is all of the plants and animals in an area. It includes the air, water, and soil too.

BIG ANIMALS WITH BIG ROLES

Elephants change the land where they live. Imagine you are in a grassland. Look! A herd of elephants walks by.

The elephants make paths in the grass. They knock over young trees. They eat the leaves and roots. This helps the grassland stay healthy. Without elephants, the land would be covered with trees.

Elephants keep forests healthy too. They make trails. They also make clearings. Elephants peel the bark off trees. The trees die. A small clearing forms. Sunlight shines through. Young trees will begin to grow. This keeps the forest strong.

Changing the Land.
Elephants are big animals. They change the places where they live.

Grassland Giants.
Elephants help keep grasslands healthy.

Clearing the Way.
An elephant uses its tusks to make a clearing in the forest.

Most of Africa is made up of flat land. There are few mountains. Deserts cover the northern and southern parts of the continent. Rain forests grow along the Equator. Grasslands called savannas fill most of the remaining land.

Elephant Population

We are not sure how many elephants live in Africa. It is hard for humans to travel through the wilderness to find the animals. The counts we have are just good guesses, or estimates.

Questions

1. Look at the map. In what land regions do most African elephants live?

2. Look at the population chart below. In which area of Africa are population counts the least definite? Why do you think that is?

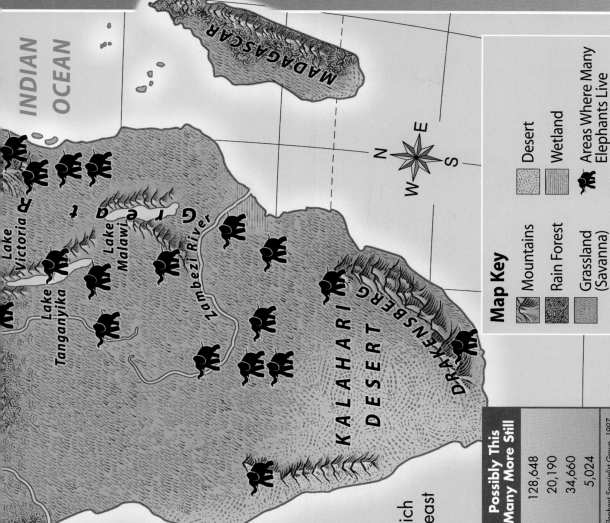

INDIAN OCEAN

MADAGASCAR

Lake Victoria
Lake Tanganyika
Lake Malawi
Great Rift
Zambezi River
KALAHARI DESERT
DRAKENSBERG

N E S W

Map Key

Mountains	Desert
Rain Forest	Wetland
Grassland (Savanna)	Areas Where Many Elephants Live

MAP/MARTIN WALZ   ILLUSTRATION/STUART ARMSTRONG

Area	Definitely This Many	Probably This Many More	Possibly This Many More Still
Central Africa	7,320	81,657	128,648
Eastern Africa	90,292	16,707	20,190
Southern Africa	170,120	16,382	34,660
Western Africa	2,771	1,282	5,024

Source: International Union for Conservation of Nature and Natural Resources/African Elephant Specialist Group, 1997

Elephants

Answer these questions to find out what you learned about elephants.

1 What kinds of things might elephants say to one another?

2 Why do elephants use infrasound?

3 How do people study infrasound?

4 Why are elephants in danger of dying out?

5 How do elephants change the places where they live?